A PATHWAY TO INNER PEACE:

A Devotional Especially for the Busy Young Adults

By

Bernice Ighele Odudu

Table of Contents

Dedication

This book is dedicated in everlasting Memory of my beloved brother-in-law Rev. Fr, Louis Odudu.

March 20th, 1960 -September 19th, 2018.

When God calls you to service He gives you the Grace to accomplish it.

Rev Fr. Louis Odudu was called. He accepted the call and dedicated his life to the service of Humanity.

Acknowledgments

My acknowledgment to all those whose books, articles, and sermons have inspired me to compile this devotional pathway to inner peace, especially for young adults. I may have been unable to reach most of you during the compilation. I, therefore, ask for your indulgence in any acknowledgment of error. Ms. Abigail Israel also assisted with the review. To Bishop Charles and Rev. Carol Ighele of Holy Spirit mission Inc and all the priests who served in my parish, whose teachings have been a source of inspiration. To my husband James and my children Dorothy, Benedict, and Paul, whose busy lives spurred me to assist them in their daily struggles. Most of the text in this devotional was extracted from daily text messages shared with the children, their cousins, and friends to help with the spiritual and emotional chaos each day brings. Above all, the Almighty God, without whom this devotional would not have been completed.

About the Author

Bernice Ighele-Odudu is a philanthropist and an ambassador to St. Yves Children Foundation. She is a registered nurse of over thirty years. She is a mother, wife, and sister to ten siblings. She holds a Master of Science in Nursing/Education. She has mentored numerous student nurses during her career as an adjunct faculty. She coaches immigrant and new grad nurses struggling with the challenges of navigating the healthcare system. She is passionate about helping young people achieve their God-giving potential.

Introduction

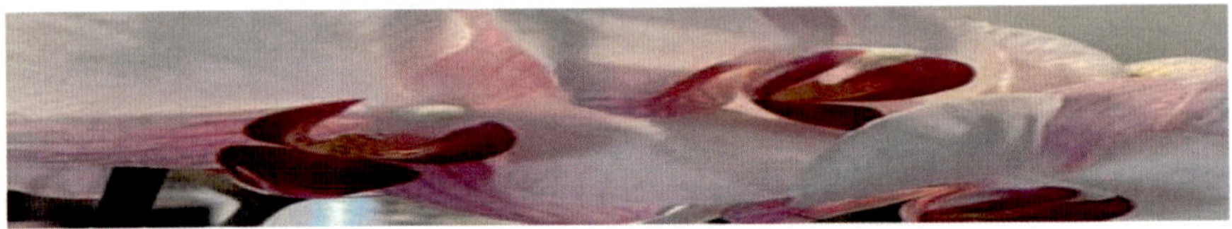

This devotional pathway is specially dedicated to the busy young adult who feels deeply overwhelmed with challenges encountered each day and sometimes thinks adulthood is a scam. The daily text will help deal with the inner struggles, cultural shock, fears, and anxieties in a rapidly changing worldview. This devotional pathway is geared towards helping each one to embrace the inner peace of God through deliberate effort and come to the ultimate realization that setbacks are not meant to break us but to make us. They are nothing but stepping stones to a better future.

My prayer for all young adults is that each genuinely finds that pathway to inner peace in their daily endeavors. Parents will find it useful as a resource for encouraging their struggling family members. Sharing with them daily via text messages may help ignite in them a lasting pathway to inner peace.

Day One

Psalm 3: 4

"I cried unto the LORD with my voice, and HE heard me out of HIS holy hill. Selah".

What a reassuring revelation. The human mind cannot grasp or explain life's experiences and suffering; only God can. Therefore, we ought to accept this by faith; then, only can it become a stepping stone to glory. Sometimes we are faced with difficulties that break us and torment our whole being. Tears from affliction and broken hearts tend to blind us from seeing the saving power of God. In situations such as financial crisis, illness, death of loved ones, and disappointment, it is only by observing the Word of God that we can rediscover HIS power and love. If only we could gear our minds and thoughts towards obedience to the will of the Father, we would be sure to experience inner peace. So let us stretch out our hands and open our hearts today to embrace the love of God. Together let us take steps towards observing His words so we can receive peace within us. As we Echo the words of the Psalmist, we might find ourselves infecting others along the way with our testimonies and joy emanating from our answered prayer.

Let Us Pray.

Dear God, forgive me for the many times I have gone astray and failed to recognize your saving power. In my affliction (mention the situation), I have tried to do it on my own. I resolve today to observe your words. My hands are stretched out to you for your saving grace. May my testimony release the fragrance of joy and peace into my heart and mind and that of anyone I will interact with today.

Amen 

Day Two

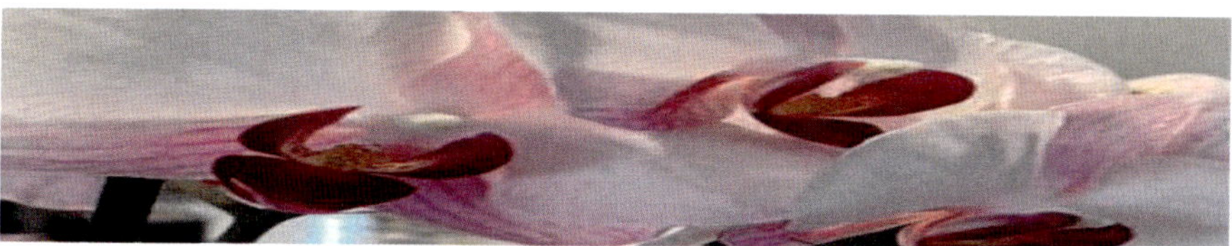

Isaiah 49:11:

'And make all my mountain a way, and my highways shall be exalted.'

You and I often have mountains that threaten to break us at certain points in our lives. We pray and wish they are removed. Mountains are obstacles that are meant to build us and maybe answers to the very thing we are praying for. They make us tougher, strengthen our inner man, and act as stepping stones on our way up.

Would you just give up on an intruder without a fight? Of course not! We will kick, punch, bleed, fall, and get back up, again and again, to stay in the fight. In the same way, we should not give up on situations that tend to threaten our inner peace. Be it disappointment in a career we wished for, suffering from a genetic condition, a sour relationship, or heartbreak. Whatever that situation may be, God has promised to make a way out. With such reassurance from our father, we must not be discouraged when ominous mountains seem to threaten our existence. We must stand firm and put up a spiritual fight; with prayer, fasting, and faith, the much-needed victory will surely come.

Let Us Pray.

Dear God, forgive me for the many times I have been so frustrated in the situation I find myself in.

Give me the grace to recognize that what I am worrying and so frustrated about serves to make me stronger and will ultimately lead to my success.

Heal me, my family members, friends, and colleagues of all the frustrations encountered today. In Jesus's Name.

Amen 

Day Three

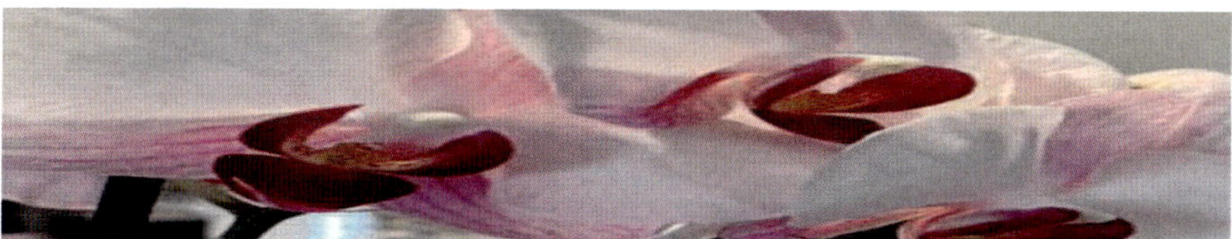

Psalm 78:72:

'He guides them by the skillfulness of his hands.'

Are you in doubt as to the way to go? The scripture says our God guides our every step. Our answer will surely come when we submit our judgment absolutely to the will of God. We must ask him to shut against us every door but the right one and keep forging ahead, considering the absence of direction, to be that of God. As you go, you will find that he is leading you to the door of opportunity, which is broader and deeper than you can imagine.

God often guides us through difficulties in our daily lives. At some point, the way may be so dark that we cannot see any way out. Nevertheless, as we wait, we notice some strange or even ordinary incidents unfold which make absolutely no sense. These may be repeated in dreams, revelation from others, and sermons in answer to our prayers.

Let's Us Pray.

Dear God, forgive me for the many times I have failed to see your guiding hand in my life and try to control my life and that of others.

Give me the Spirit of trust, and show me the chart of your purpose for my life. Help me to go forward cheerfully, trusting in your will concerning my life today.

In Jesus Christ's Name. Amen 

Thank you, Lord.

Day Four

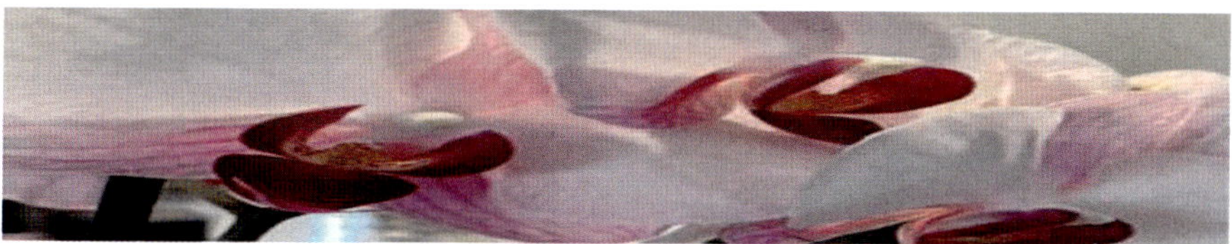

Mathew 25 v 1-13

'....Whereas the sensible, wise ones took the flask of oil in their lamps.......'

Reading this Bible story brought these images to mind:

The five sensible ones were prepared. They took not only their lamps but an extra flask of oil. Why? Just in case the oil in the lamp burns out

They also fell asleep. With the spare flask of oil, they had the confidence to get some sleep knowing fully well that they had a refill. As a result, they were well-rested. They were physically and mentally ready to welcome the Bridegroom on His arrival.

These girls took care of their whole being.

The oil is very significant. It did not only keep the lamp burning, but it also illuminated and brightened the arena. It exuded comfort! There was visibility! They could finally see the bridegroom as He really was when he arrived.

We can strive to be like the five sensible girls in this Bible reading. Just like the girls, we need to care for our holistic health daily. This includes:

1. Physical health: which involves exercise and nutrition.

2. Emotional health: Maintaining emotional stability.

3. Mental health: Exercising our mind. Weeding out any problem which takes more than 30 minutes of our daily thoughts. Taking time to sleep and resting our mental state.

4. Spiritual: Dwelling on things that are uplifting to our souls, such as music, arts, and books; prayer, fasting, and faith will help us focus on God.

When our spiritual lamps are not only filled with oil but have some in reserve, we will be prepared for any disappointment, discouragement, and frustrations encountered by the other five foolish girls who had no spare flask of oil. Their lamps burned out, and they had to go in search of oil in the darkness of night. On their return, the bridegroom had arrived, and the door was shut against them. You can imagine their plight. Their agony will never be our portion in Jesus's Name.

Let Us Pray.

Dear God, forgive me for the many times I have failed to have a spare flask of oil in my daily life.

I commit my physical, emotional, spiritual, and relational well-being into your hands. Free me from discouragement and frustrations tormenting me and the life of any of my loved ones today, in Jesus's Name.

Amen 

Day Five

Luke 24:14

'And they talked together of all these things which had happened.'

Sometimes we find ourselves in situations in life that are difficult to understand, just like these two disciples. Jesus was said to have been seen by some of the disciples after they witnessed the horrific crucifixion. They were confused, disappointed, and had no idea what to make of all the rumors about the resurrection of Jesus.

Perhaps, we, too, might have found ourselves in similar situations when we could not understand what was happening and going forward seemed impossible. Despite being surrounded by social media, friends, and family, we still feel distant, sad, and frustrated and just want to go somewhere by ourselves, just like these two disciples on their way to Emmaus. We withdraw into ourselves and shut the doors and our hearts. The sleepless nights, gazing at the walls and ceilings, speak volumes of the pain we bear.

Then, suddenly, an unusual situation happens; a flicker of light in the dark guides you out into happier moments. Just as Jesus suddenly appeared to these dejected and discouraged disciples. Yes, you can physically feel in your soul the gentle hand of the Savior and hear His voice whispering, "My child, it is I! Let me explain; let me show you." Suddenly your eyes and mind open as you take the difficulty to the Father and yield to His will. Your footsteps are quickened. You become lighter. God guides us through lonely times because His plan is better than ours.

Let Us Pray.

Dear God, forgive me for the many times I failed to yield to your will when lonely and broken. Thank you for the times you have led me through the darkest path. I ask for your helping hand of grace upon me, my brothers, sisters, cousins, and parents who are going through any dark situation at this time.

In Jesus's Name, I pray.

Amen 

Day Six

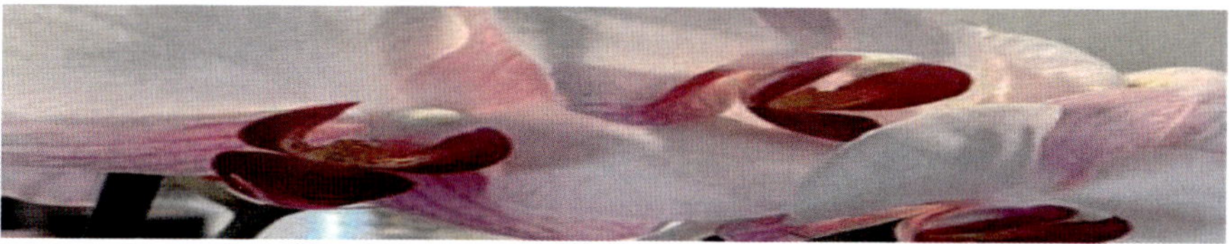

Deuteronomy 1: 8

'Look …………. I have given you, go and take possession.'

The word 'LOOK' is very significant. To look is to consider more closely or have a better view of an object or a situation. In this passage, God is telling us to look again and again until we begin to see it differently and feel steering within us. A shout of 'Yes, I can, or Yes, We can' echoes from within. What is that situation which seems to drain you of all your strength? That dream job you have been denied or the business plan, which is not breaking through (no funding, no sponsor).

Hear this story: A young lady accidentally dropped her purse, and a beggar found it. When the beggar tried to draw the lady's attention, he was churned and ridiculed; out of pride, the young lady refused to acknowledge the beggar and did not collect her purse. She did not want to be seen in the company of such a dirty person. She left without her purse, and as the beggar was contemplating what to do, something within him prompted him to look inside the purse. He looked and found some money and a piece of paper with these words written on it" I can become great if I work hard." The beggar clutched the piece of paper to his heart. He used the money to start a hawking business, from which he became a car dealer. The story ended with the same young lady showing up to rent a car from this former beggar's office for an engagement. The beggar recognized the lady and introduced himself. This time the lady listened.

Had the beggar tossed the purse and not looked inside closely, he might have missed his opportunity to start on a new trajectory. God is telling you today to look again and again and that He has provided all that it takes to bring that dream of yours to reality. But you must look first and not fret.

Let Us Pray.

Dear God, forgive me for the many times I have failed to look and fretted instead. Steer up my spiritual eyes to look again and again until I can see the brighter days You planned for me.

In Jesus's Name, I pray.

Amen 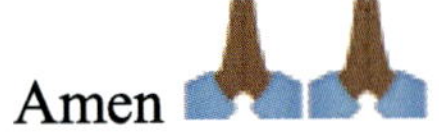

Day Seven

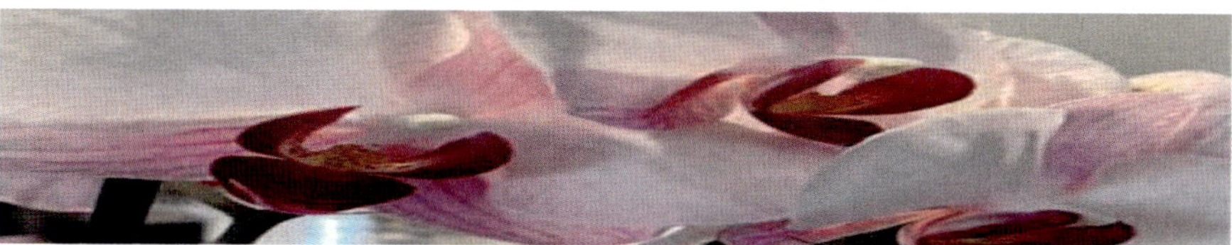

Luke 16:9

'Make to yourself Friends.'

This text came after the story of the dishonest servant who was about to be stripped of his stewardship. This servant did not want to lose the favor of his master and that of the people, so he did an unusual thing: He went about reducing substantially the debts of those owing his master. His expectation was that the debtors would support him when he was dismissed.

What type of friends are we keeping? Will they lead and applaud us to hell or heaven.? Sometimes, we befriend people because of their status or what they can do for us and disregard their character. There is a saying that 'birds of the same feathers flock together.' The company of friends we keep influences our thoughts and way of life. Often, we leave our family values and inculcate those of friends because we yearn for their acceptance.

Beware! Friends can affect you positively or negatively.

The story is told of a young girl from a well-known Christian family who had friends at school whose families were into the drug business and usage. She would often spend time at their homes and soon got introduced to doing drugs. Over time, she became addicted to the point that she dropped out of school because of the psychotic behavior induced by the drugs. She is currently in a rehabilitation center. Her family is devasted and living in the shame and guilt of being tagged as incompetent parents. There are countless stories of this nature out there.

Friends may mean a lot to us, but we must choose them wisely. Yes, there are also positive stories of friends who have led others to know the love of God. Let us choose friends that will influence us positively.

Let Us Pray.

Dear God, please lead me to friends who are true to your word; friends that will help to increase my knowledge of Christ and compassion for people; Friends with whom, together, we can make the world better than we met it.

In Jesus's Name Amen 

Day Eight

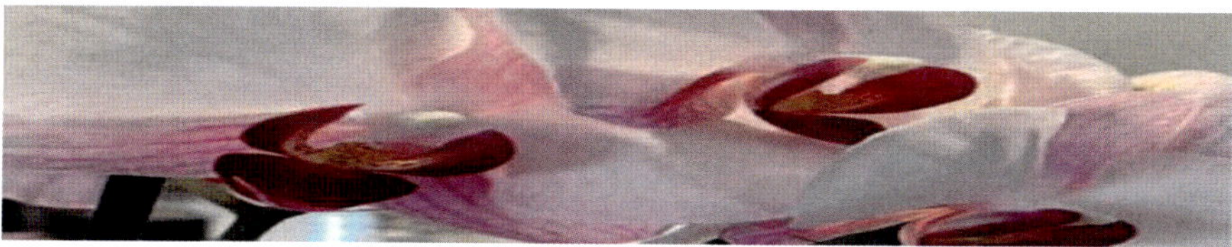

Jeremiah 1: 17

'As for you prepare yourself for action…. Have no fear of them. In their presence, I will make you fearless'.

Hmm ……. what divine instruction and reassurance? To prepare is to have a plan for a challenge ahead. You and I often have well-thought-out plans for our day-to-day challenges. Most times, they are very good plans for the ears and for all those who read them, but there is often a lingering feeling of doubt and fear. Questions race through our minds "What if it does not work? How will I face people? I will become a laughingstock! We are plagued by these thoughts because we do not want to be considered as being incapable.

Here, this passage is telling us to go beyond being prepared and overcoming our fears. You and I may be going through some challenges right now. Perhaps your world is crumbling because you have just received a termination letter, or your company has filed for bankruptcy and is planning to lay off workers; Maybe the business is not having a breakthrough, and the love for your fiancée or newlywed has suddenly gone sour, or the new baby has a genetic condition. There is a lot going on. A lot of uncertainties, and you are terrified!

Today, God is saying that no matter how gigantic the problem may be, He will make us fearless in its very presence. We only must follow His instructions and be prepared for action. At such times, the armor of truth, a banquet of divine grace, and a seat of wisdom may be what is required to be prepared.

Let Us Pray.

Dear God, thank you for the many times you have prepared me and made me fearless in the face of challenges.

Open my heart to the divine amour of truth and grace. Grant me the wisdom to go through this situation.

In Jesus's Name, I pray. Amen 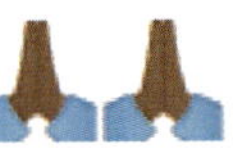

Day Nine

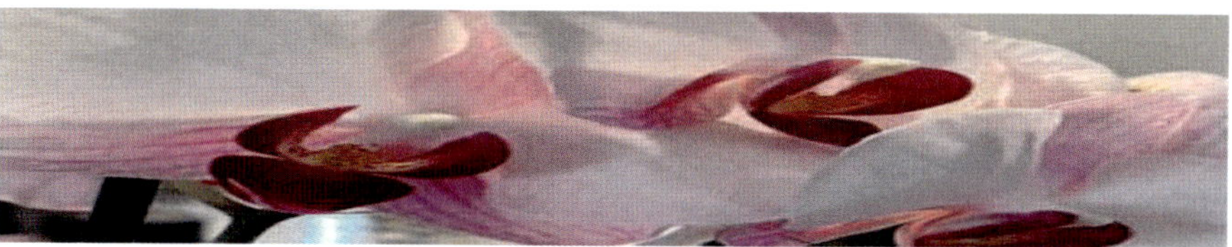

Galatians 5:5

'For we through the Spirit by faith wait for the hope of righteousness.'

Hope is waiting even when there is no glimmer of light on the horizon and yet, refusing to be discouraged or fall into despair. Hoping in the darkest time. Job was still full of hope when there was nothing left of him; When Abraham was tested to sacrifice his son Isaac, he had no idea where God had asked him to go, but he went ahead anyway. To Jesus, it all seemed very dark in Gethsemane. They all saw no ray of light, but they hoped. You may be going through that divorce; child custody battle; hateful colleagues; or frustration in your dream career. All you must do today is ask God to increase your faith. This will help strengthen your hope as you wait for the appointed time. Through the Spirit of faith, Job received back double his lost possessions; Abraham got a ram to sacrifice in place of his son, and Jesus had resurrection power. We can today ask God to increase our faith.

Let Us Pray.

God, empower me today with your Divine power of Faith and Hope. Grant me the grace to wait in Hope at this time and moment; when all is so dark, and the joy I expect seems gone. Give me the power to stand unconquered by this situation.

Give me the strength to say, "in the eyes of my Father, this too shall pass. God will show up in this situation, not before or after.

In Jesus's Name, I pray.

Amen 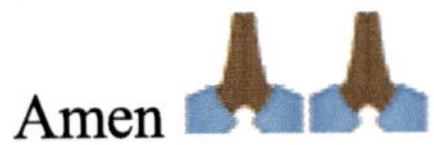

Day Ten

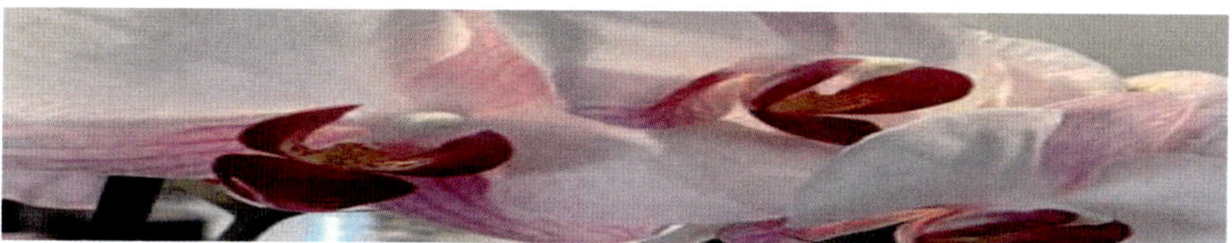

Psalm 71 V 1-2

'In your saving justice, rescue me deliver me …. Listen to me and save me.'

We often echo this cry for help when in a crisis and the human solution seems far off.

I heard this story over the radio about a lady whose daughter was seriously ill. While rushing to pick up the prescription from the pharmacy, she accidentally locked her keys in the car.

On returning to the car, she couldn't find the keys to open the door. As she searched desperately for the keys in her purse, she spotted them inside the locked car. All attempts to open the car failed, and no one was in sight to help. She started praying for God to send someone to her rescue. Suddenly an unkempt man on a motorcycle pulled up beside her. She was scared and started asking God if this was the help He had sent. She summoned up courage and told the man of her predicament. The man proceeded to help her, and in less than two minutes, the door of the car was open. The lady was overjoyed and jumped and hugged the man saying, 'You are an angel.' The man said, 'No, I am not.' 'Yes, you are, the lady insisted. The man responded, 'No, I can't be an angel because I was jailed for breaking into a car. I just got out. I was released two hours ago. I can't be an angel'

This story made me wonder how God might have sent me help which I failed to recognize. God always shows up to help in times of need, not after or before. This situation that is frustrating your life right now has an answer right beside you from an unexpected source and person. Ask God so you can recognize it.

Let Us Pray.

Dear God, forgive me for the many times I have failed to recognize the help you sent my way. Please open the eyes of my Heart to recognize the help you sent to my family members and me today.

Amen 

Day Eleven

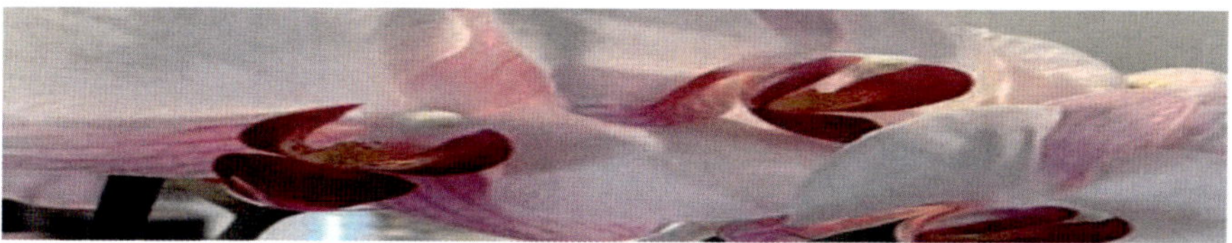

Number 21: 4

'…And the soul of the people was much discouraged because of the way.'

The Israelites were on their way to the promised land, and a place said to be flowing with milk and honey. According to the scriptures, God performed many miracles and wonders before their eyes; the plagues on Pharaoh and the Egyptians; the parting of the red sea; the provision of water from the rock, manna as food in the middle of nowhere, and the destruction of enemy nations on the way. Despite these miracles, the Israelites still got discouraged and were always complaining.

You and I are not different from the Israelites. We get discouraged when things do not go our way. We complain about everything except ourselves. Have you lost patience with that dream, that career, the stagnant business, or your relationship? God gave you His Son on the cross so you can look on Him and be saved from despair and eternal death, just like the bronze serpent was lifted on the pole in the wilderness by Moses. All that looked on it were healed from the poisonous snake bite. We must therefore find a way to get to the cross and look upon Him who was crucified for us to liberate us from discouragement and despair.

Take time today to listen to the lyrics of Blessing Offor's song, 'Brighter Days' It will soothe your discouraged and ailing Spirit and get your thoughts refocused on better days ahead.

Let Us Pray.

Dear God, forgive me for the many times I have lost patience because things did not go my way. Direct my inner eyes to look at the Man on the cross so I can be free from discouragement and despair. Create a glorious harmony in my life from this day. In Jesus Name

Amen 

Day Twelve

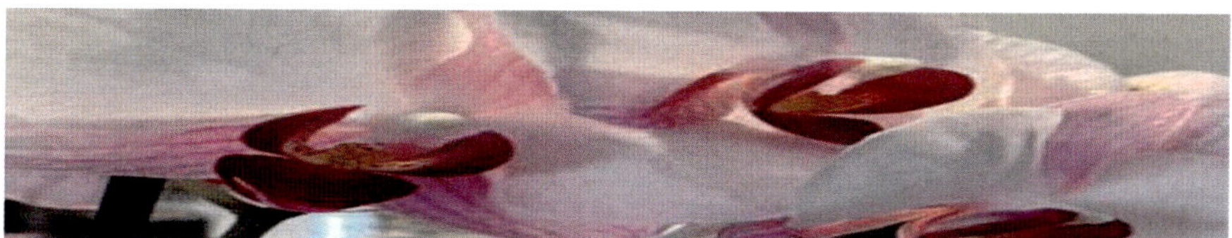

Mark 10: 51

'What will thou that I should do unto you.'

This intriguing story was about Bartimaeus, the blind man who sat begging on the road leading out of Jericho as Jesus was passing by. Bartimaeus must have heard beautiful things about Jesus, His love, compassion, and miracles. Perhaps he must have been imagining what these Jesús, whom everyone was talking about, looked like. This day, Bartimaeus positioned himself in a strategic place by the roadside, where his voice could be heard. As soon as he heard the crowd, perhaps shouting the name of Jesus, he knew Jesus was certainly close by. What did Bartimaeus do? He made sure his voice was the loudest among the surging crowd. Verse 49 states, 'many charged him that he should hold his peace,' but he shouted even louder to draw Jesus's attention. Jesus heard his voice and asked that he be brought to Him.

Jesus knew what Bartimaeus wanted, but the crowd probably thought being a blind beggar, what he needed was some money to meet his daily need. Bartimaeus desperately needed something different and permanent. And when Jesus posed the question to him, 'What will thou I should do unto you,' he did not hesitate to say, "I need my sight, I just want to see, I do not want to beg anymore."

Are you at that kind of crossroads? Maybe you are so frustrated that your whole world is crashing down. And you keep saying to yourself, "I do not know what to do. I just can't think straight, 'I am so confused.' Let Jesus hear you shout above those voices, saying, 'you can't get out of this mess.' He is standing by you right now. Just like

Bartimaeus, ask Jesus to have mercy on you today. He will shut down the crowd and bring you to his side and give you what you truly need!

Let Us Pray.

Dear God, I am sorry for the many times I have failed to shut out the voices of hopelessness. Please help me, like Bartimaeus, to persevere amid opposing voices, to be heard by you as you bid me come into your presence. Heal me of all the confusion that clouds my being today.

In Jesus's Name, I pray

Amen 

Day Thirteen

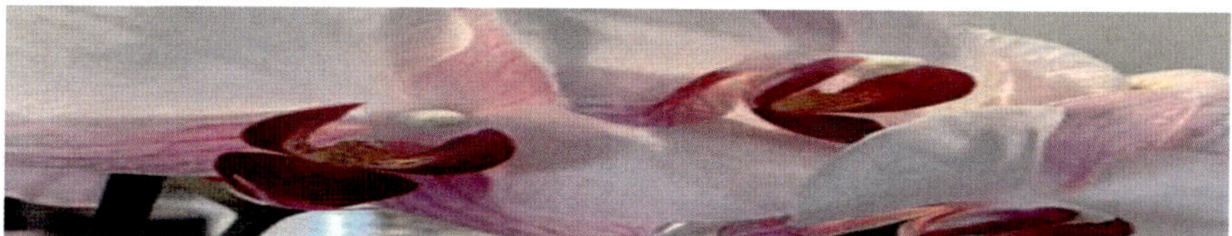

2 Thessalonian 3: 10

'…If anyone will not work, neither should He eat.'

This admonition was from Paul to the church in Thessalonica. Paul was the greatest evangelist of his time. Often, he encouraged the congregation on the importance of work. He always worked to meet his personal needs so as not to place a burden on members of the early church

Today, social influencers have a new message for the youth, "Work less" or "You do not need to work 9 to 5" You can stay at home, and your money will work for you." We hear stories of how their multimillion-dollar businesses were started in their garage, backyard, or living room. However, they fail to tell us the many obstacles they encountered and the adjustment and sacrifices they had to make. Let's ask ourselves some basic questions. 'Can one start a business without a plan and capital as a college student or new graduate? 'Absolutely not. We do, however, have to start with some form of work to save money for the business or to invest in stock or whatever new way of making money on the internet. We should never be deceived by today's sugar-coated messages flooding the internet, and these only serve to derail us. Some of us have distanced ourselves from family and friends who told us the truth about the "influencers world' and the real world. We are so ashamed to retrace our steps, and we want TO PROVE we were right. So, we fall into depression, drugs, and marijuana and are at loggerheads with anyone who tries to encourage us to see the truth.

You, reading this, maybe in this situation or know someone who is. God is giving you and me new hope. We can start a meaningful job today. We can begin to set aside a certain percentage of our income to invest in our dream business after we have paid all our bills. Paul is telling us today to take our life back to a place of inner peace.

Let Us Pray.

Dear God, forgive me for the many times I have failed to work but still want all the pleasures of life. Help me to seek a meaningful job and open my eyes, heart, and mind to embrace the inner peace which comes from a humble beginning. Bless the work of my hands and prosper me in this land where you have brought me.

In Jesus's Name, I pray. Amen 

Day Fourteen

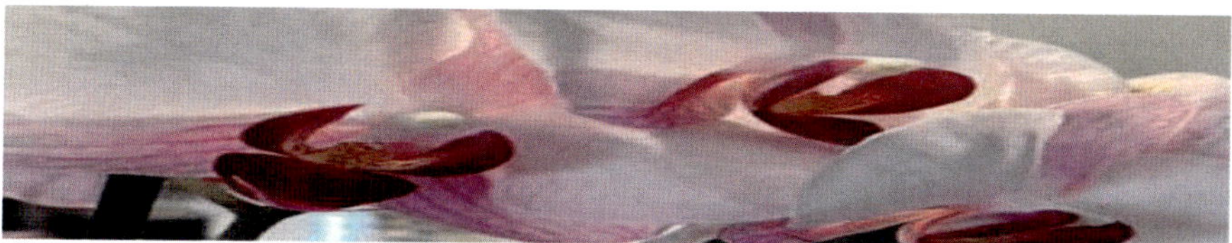

Psalm 24: 4

"He that hath clean hands, pure hearts, who hath not lifted up his soul unto vanity nor sworn deceitfully.'

The above text is an answer to the question posed in Psalm 24: 3. 'Who shall ascend into the hill of the Lord? Or who shall stand in His Holy place? Are we qualified to stand in the Lord's presence? Are our hands and heart clean and pure enough? Do we embrace that which is not biblically correct? Or do we lust for material wealth? Do we take that which is meant for others? Or do we participate in unholy talks and gatherings?

If we are desperate to enjoy His presence, we must reexamine our lives and embark on a deliberate quest to do that which is right and acceptable to God,

Let Us Pray

Dear God, create in me a clean heart. May God the father, God the son, and God the Holy Spirit guide my thoughts and actions. Oh, let me not be satisfied until my whole being is flooded with your presence and infinite love.

In Jesus's Name

Amen 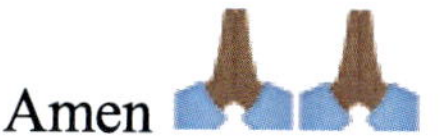

Day Fifteen

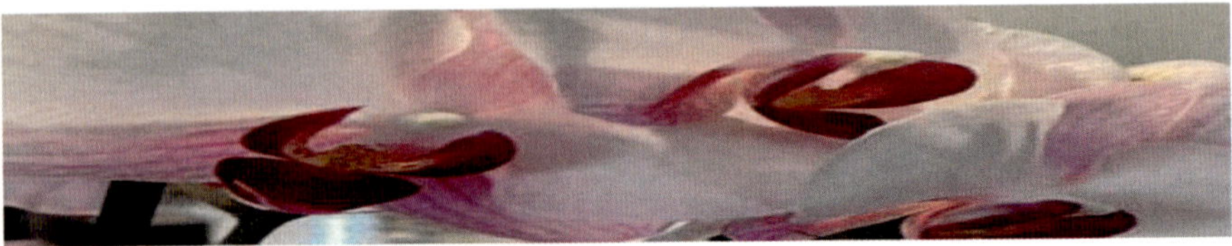

Acts 2: 4

'And they were filled with the Holy Spirit and began to speak in tongues as the Spirit gave utterance.'

The book of Acts, which describes the early church's encounter with the Holy Spirit, gives us an insight into what transpired. When the Holy Spirit rested on them, they were transformed from ordinary people to Christ-like heavenly glorious beings. The Holy Spirit gave each one of them new utterances and the fruits of the Spirit, which are Love, Joy, Peace, Patience, Kindness, Goodness, Faithfulness, Gentleness, and Self-Control. This means these fruits must manifest in our lives before we can find inner peace. Can you imagine what our lives would be if we had these fruits as part of our daily life?

The Baptism of the Holy Spirit comes with its fruits. Therefore, any situation which makes you lash out at others, become agitated and produces suicidal thoughts, and destructive behavior, should not have a place in your daily life.

Let Us Pray.

Father God, let the light of your Holy Spirit shine into my heart and soul as you awaken my inner man. Break the chains of darkness, misunderstanding, and confusion tormenting my life today. Let, Love, Joy, Peace, Patience, Kindness, Goodness, Faithfulness, Gentleness, and Self-Control guide my everyday action.

Amen 

Day Sixteen

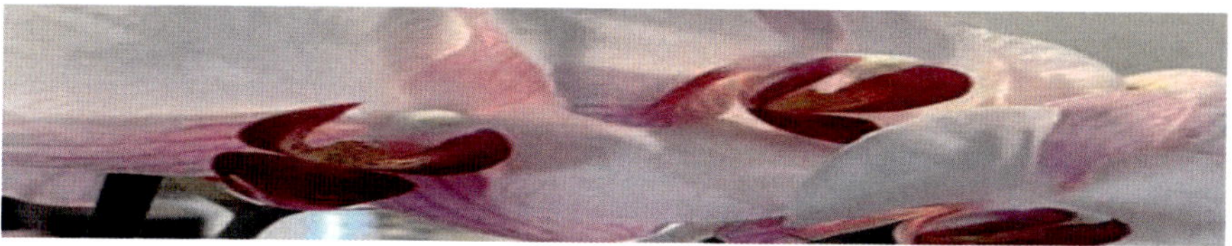

Isaiah 40: 30.

'Even the youths shall faint and be weary, and the young men shall utterly fall.'

Everyone who has walked this planet has, at certain times in their lives, been weary in the soul and fainted. All have sinned. Do not be deceived. We all have been through the same pathway at some point in our lives. Perhaps, you are feeling hopeless and powerless in the grip of that addiction and are angry at everything around you. There is good news for you today! Hear this: You can overcome any situation if you make a deliberate effort.

Isaiah 40: 29 & 31 gives us an insight into this new hope. God has promised to give us power and strength if we wait on Him. Let us heed His voice today and seek Him. Through prayers and fasting, burdens will be lifted and yokes destroyed. God did not promise to take away our pain, but he never stopped giving us the grace we needed to go through it.

Let Us Pray.

All-powerful God, I am filled with anxieties and worries about today (Mention them). Please grant me and all others going through turbulent times the strength and power to overcome every situation. I will proclaim your goodness and greatness forever.

In Jesus's Name, I pray

Amen 

Day Seventeen

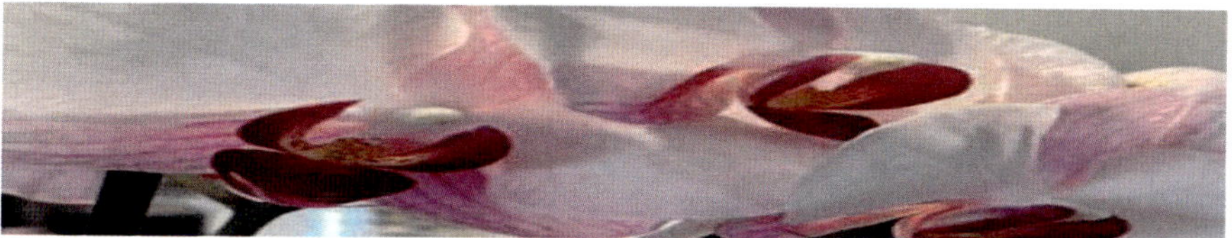

Philippians 4: 19

'But my God shall supply all your needs according to the riches of his glory by Christ Jesus.'

Each day, we find ourselves in dire need of one thing or the other. You certainly must have prayed and perhaps done all that is humanly possible to meet that need with no sign of success. The story was once told of a young man whose father died when he was ten years old. Left with his mother and only brother, life became very difficult. His mother then died when he turned twenty-two, leaving him with his brother. After a while, the brother moved away to the city, and they both lost touch. The young man found himself alone. He struggled to get through university with the help of some good people. After graduation, getting a good-paying job became a challenge. Through the years, the young man was always prayerfully reminding God each day to help with his daily needs. Each time God showed up for him, providing food, clothes, fees, and relationships. This stirred up his zeal for God and his way of life. One day he went for an interview with a well-known corporate organization. As the CEO was browsing through his resume, the last name rang a bell in his memory. He once knew a man with that name. He asked the young man if he was in any way related to that person. The young man replied that he was his father. It happened that the CEO and this young man's father were childhood friends. What followed was a miracle. He was offered a high-paying job in the organization. The young man's life was completely turned around. Within six months, he had a well-furnished house and a brand-new car, as well as a company car. When God shows up, there certainly is a turnaround.

Hmm. Maybe you are like the young man just surviving from day to day. Do not despair. God knows where you are at. He is telling you, 'WAIT, I will show you that I am with you.'

Let Us Pray.

Dear God, I thank you for meeting my basic needs. I believe that this situation also shall pass. I will be happier if you say 'YES' now, but let you will be done.

In Jesus's Name, I pray. Amen 

Day Eighteen

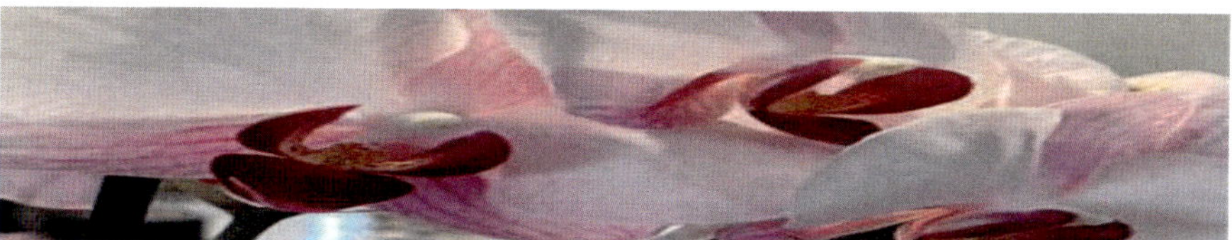

Luke 6:8

'Rise up and stand forth in the midst.

This beautiful story in the scriptures has several layers. The scribes and Pharisees were watching closely to see if Jesus would heal somebody on the Sabbath. They were looking for an occasion to bring charges against him. For the Jews, the Sabbath is a day of rest in which no work ought to be done. Jesus perceived their thoughts and beckoned to the man with the withered hand, saying, 'Rise up and stand forth in the midst. What did Jesus do? He asked the man to stretch out his hand, and the withered hand received new flesh, muscles, ligaments, and nerves. HALLELUJAH!

The man with the withered hand was probably not the only disabled person in the crowd, but Jesus spotted him and singled him out. Today you may be suffering in some way. Jesus has spotted you in the crowd. He is asking you to stand up in the presence of all those who have scorned and ridiculed you in the past because of your situation. He is about to show His saving power. You must recognize and obey what He has asked you to do. There will be no more depression, mental stress, inattentiveness, and sleeplessness. Yeah! You are free! Free!

Let Us Pray.

Dear God, forgive me for the many times I have gone astray and plunged deeper into defiling your name by my addiction and immoral behavior. I yield to your voice to stand up amid my situation. I am on my knees. Deliver me from this addiction and any situation which has separated me from you in the presence of those who scorn me.

In Jesus's Name, I pray. Amen 

Day Nineteen

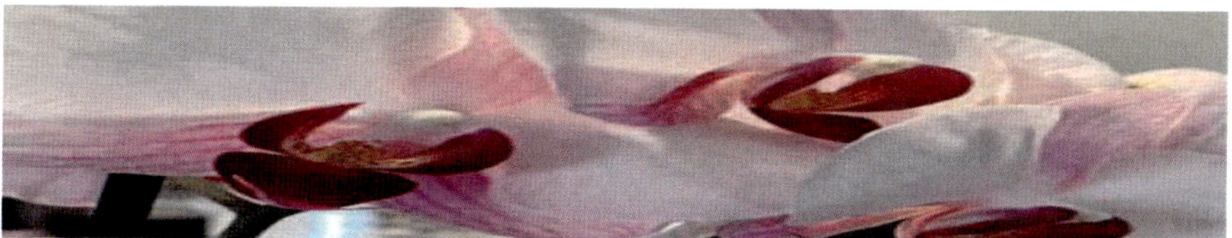

Genesis 28:15

'And behold, I am with thee. And will keep thee in all places whither thou go ………… until I have done that which I have spoken to thee of.

What a reassurance! Imagine hearing such comforting words from a friend or father who cares deeply for you. What are you supposed to do? Stay in the same place, ignore them, and continue to wallow in mystery? God says He is with you. Then, now, and after. He promised to keep you and me safe wherever we go and will never forsake us.

There was a story of this family who lost their father in a motor accident three months prior. The mother and her two sons were in the living room praying when the smell of smoke broke through. They found the kitchen on fire. To make things worse, the only exit was by the kitchen, where the fire was raging. They managed to make it out with minor burns but lost all their possession before the firemen showed up. They had nowhere to go. No clothes! No money! A neighbor was able to house them for the first week, after which they moved from one shelter to the other. One day, one of the staff at the shelter heard their story and decided to share it on 'Go Fund Me.' In less than twenty-four hours, one hundred thousand dollars was raised, including furniture, clothes, and household items. They were able to get an apartment and, three months later, purchased a brand-new home.

This is God fulfilling the above promise in the life of this family. His promises are forever sure. For those who have faith in Him, God will not only show up, but He will also position people in their lives who will provide the help needed in any situation.

Let Us Pray.

Dear God, forgive me the many times I have been blind to your saving grace. I believe you will meet me in this situation as you met this

family. In Jesus's Name. Amen 

Day Twenty

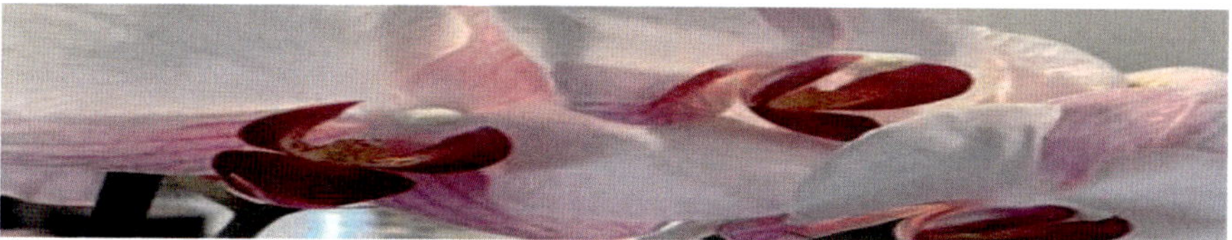

Ephesians 4: 29

'Let no corrupt communication proceed out of your mouth, but that which is good to the use of edifying, that it may minister grace unto the hearers.'

While hanging out with friends and family, sometimes everyone turns on one person. The conversation gets heated. That individual is subjected to ridicule and 'trashy' comments. It could become physical, or the person may just walk away. Walking away would deny friends and family access to his emotions

The Bible passage cautions us to be mindful of what proceeds from our mouths. We may call them 'Jokes,' but they can be hurtful. They penetrate and affect the human mind. They do not impart grace. Feelings of hurt ignite the flames of agitation and destructive behavior, which are harmful to self and others. Some people have committed suicide as a result of "unwholesome talk."

The story was once told of this teacher. A student in his class could not answer a particular question correctly. The teacher got so angry and shouted at the student, "You dumb fool, sit down." The whole class busted out laughing at the student. On the way home from school that day, the student, still feeling very hurt from the aftermath of what happened earlier in class, walked absentmindedly onto an upcoming car. He was badly injured and did not survive.

Let Us Pray.

Dear God, forgive me for the many times I have indulged in unwholesome conversation which causes pain to others. Help me to choose words that will build others.

In Jesus's Name Amen 

Day Twenty-one

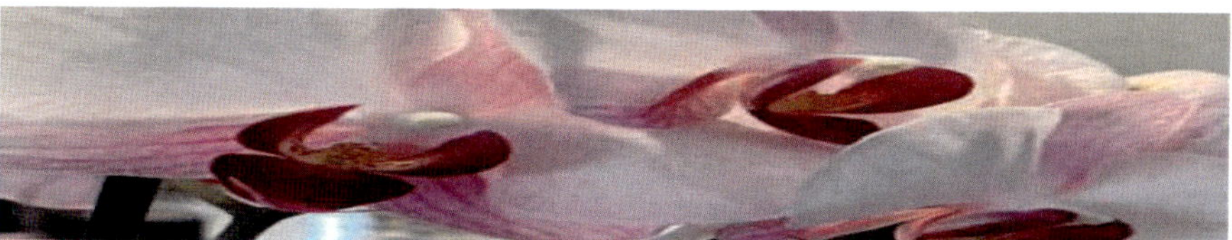

Psalm 121: 1-2

'I will lift mines eyes unto the hills from whence cometh my help

My help comes from the Lord who made heaven and earth.'

This seems to be the cry of someone who got to that place of realization of a GOD who saves. It is the sigh of relief from one who was in a valley, who may have thought there was never going to be a way out. Perhaps, it was grief from the loss of a loved one or severe sickness which has defiled all medical interventions. Heartbreak from a relationship breaks–up, frustration with that dream which seems ever so unattainable, chronic addiction, anger. Yes, these are some of the situations people may be going through today. These are terrible times.

Dear child, look up to the hill from the valley where you are right now. 'On that hill far away stands a rugged cross where a Savior is standing and waiting, the Son of the God who made heaven and earth.

Dear child, you may be wondering within you, 'Is it that simple?' Yes, it is! Open the eyes of your heart, and you will see where your help will come from. The help will certainly come from the Lord who made heaven and earth. It may be right now or maybe later; LOOK AND WAIT.

Let Us Pray.

Dear Lord, I come to you today for help in this situation of mine (Mention the situation).

Thank you, Lord, for answering my prayer.

In Jesus's Name Amen 

Day Twenty-two

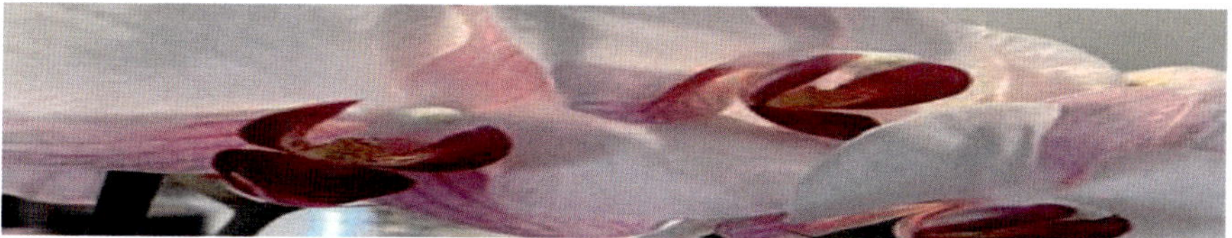

Genesis 39: 1-23

'...7. Lie with me! 9. How then can I do great wickedness and sin against God?'

The story of Joseph is very intriguing. It was very sad yet ended with double joy. Joseph was well-loved by his father because he was the son of his old age. This made some of the brothers hate him. They were even more enraged because of Joseph's dream of his brothers bowing to him. He was sold off to the Ishmaelites, who happened to be passing by while they were plotting to kill him. Joseph later ended up as a slave to Potiphar, a prominent Egyptian, who placed him in charge of his entire household. Joseph found favor with Potiphar because he was humble, dedicated, and trustworthy. Potiphar's wife got attracted to Joseph and constantly urged him to sleep with her. Joseph, off course, stood his ground. He refused to commit such a wicked act against his master, who trusted him. What happened to Joseph in the Scriptures following this decision was life-changing.

As a young person in today's world, you may be facing temptations of this sort. The question is, can you be like Joseph? Yes, you can by the grace of the Almighty.! You can resist any temptation which may come your way if you trust God as Joseph did.

Let Us Pray.

Dear Father, forgive me for the many times I have not taken a stand to be like Joseph. Pour upon me today the grace to resist all temptations which may come my way.

In Jesus's Name, I pray Amen 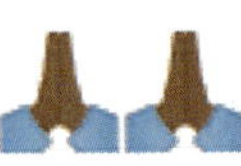

Day Twenty-Three

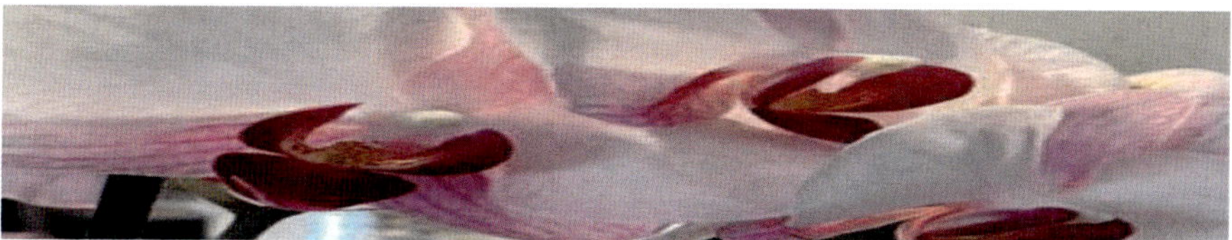

Esther: 4: 14

'For if thou altogether holdest thy peace at this time, then shall there enlargement and deliverance arise to the Jews from another place, but thou and thy father's house shall be destroyed. Who knoweth whether thou art come to the kingdom for a time as this.'

Esther summoned the courage to save the lives of Mordecai and the Jews living in Ahasuerus' entire empire at the time. Harman had plotted to destroy all the Jews because Mordecai refused to bow down to him using the King's signature seal. God turned around what Hamman had planned against the Jews. He met his own death by being hung on the gallows he had prepared for Mordecai. It took courage for Esther to say, "I will do it" 'If I perish, I perish.'

What are we doing today to save our world like Esther? Are we just contented with the status quo? Or do we say, 'It is not my business?' Hey! It is our business. If we do not take a stand today, we will all perish. You may think that remaining silent at such a time is best for you. I want to remind you today that everything we value in society is at stake. The quality of education, student loan, dream job, home ownership, vacation, healthcare, safe environment for you and your children, the beauty of technological advancement, and how and where we worship are all at stake

Do not remain indifferent because, one day, you will wake up only to realize that the freedom which you enjoy today is gone if you allow 'The Hammans' to be in control of the affairs of your country. Esther did not say,' I am too young, or 'I am content being the queen.' She took a stand to save her people. Will you be courageous to pledge to do just as Esther did? Participate in politics, vote if eligible, and promote a cause if you can. These are evil times; this is not the time to be silent. YOU and US are at stake.

Let Us Pray.

Dear God, forgive me for the many times I have been indifferent to the affairs of my country. Create in me today the Spirit to participate in any way I can for the betterment of my family, my community, my state, and my country. Do not allow the 'Hamman' of our time to succeed in their plot to impoverish us in the midst of the riches you have provided for our world.

In Jesus's Name.

Amen 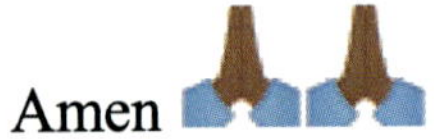

Day Twenty-Four

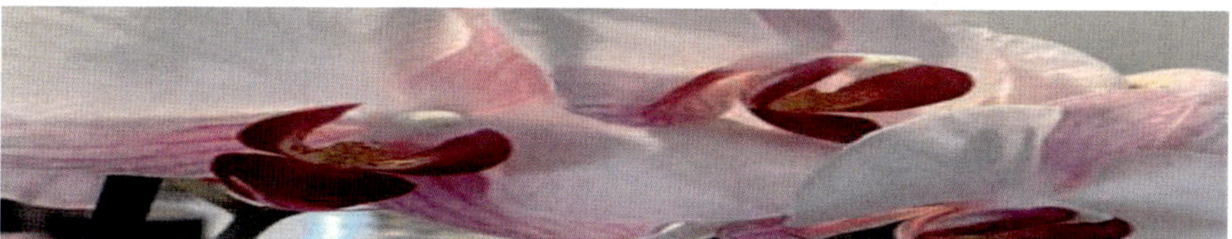

Luke 6: 40

'The disciple is not above his master. Everyone that is perfect shall be as his master.'

Often, we hear some students say,' that teacher 'sucks.' And some teachers also allude to the same to some of their students. Why is it so? This is because the teacher and the student do not fully grasp the intrinsic act and outcome of learning. A student can never be superior to the teacher, and neither the teacher to the student. The student, however, when open to learning and fully trained, may become better than the teacher.

How, then, can I become a better teacher? Our minds and hearts must be open to receiving and processing new information. In so doing, our scope of understanding opens and takes us to a place in our mind which has not yet been exploited. In research findings, a student may find the outcome of his teacher's research intriguing and may begin to have a somewhat different view. Further exploration of the new perspective may result in discovery of something of great importance to mankind. Many students who have followed this part have been propelled into the international limelight.

The student used the teacher's work as a building block for his new discovery. How was the student able to achieve this? By HUMILITY! A humble person will listen, with an open mind and heart, to the information received. He will analyze the information, filter it, and extract that which will be of benefit to himself and others. By so doing, the student liberates himself from the cocoon of the teacher's worldview. Let us learn the act of humility so we can become like or even better than our teachers.

Let Us Pray.

Dear God, I am very sorry for the many times pride has driven me away from opening my heart and mind to You and my teachers. Help me to learn the act of humility today, so I can fully understand your precepts. Bless and grant all the teachers You have placed in my trajectory the grace to provide me with sound teachings beneficial to all mankind.

In Jesus's Name, I pray.

Amen 

Day Twenty-Five

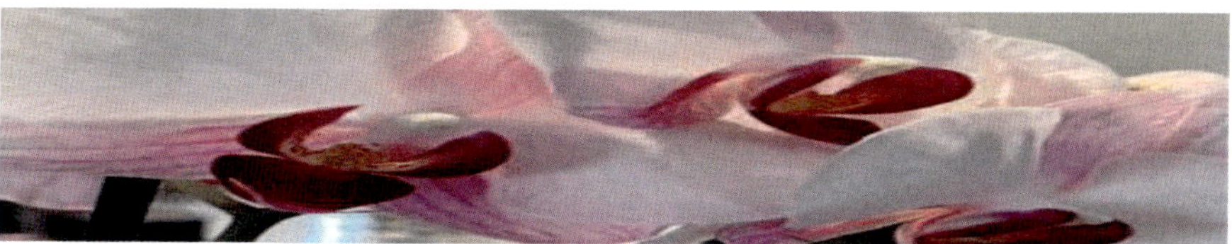

Psalm 40: 17

'But I am poor and needy; yet the Lord thinketh (remembers) upon me. Thou art my help and deliverer; make no tarrying, O my God.'

The Psalmist in the above scripture searched within his soul and realized how poor and needy he was. We live in a society that places value on our looks, what we wear, what we drive, and where we live. That is how we are defined, judged, and accepted, especially in our social media-driven world. We are constantly under pressure to showcase our achievements, and of course, sometimes, we borrow to post on social media.

Do we really need to put all that pressure on ourselves just so others can follow us on social media? NO! All that fanfare captures only a moment in our lives when all seem to be well with us.

There was the story of this famous singer who died. As well-known as he was, his profile on social media was deleted after a week. Every now and then, after that, some posts are shared about how his life influenced others. That was all that was left of him. What a world! The same is true for everyone who will depart this world. Our social media page shall be deleted too.

Let us try and echo the words of this Psalmist every moment of our lives. 'But I am poor and needy; yet the Lord thinketh (remembers) upon me. Thou art my help and deliver, make no tarrying, O my God.

Let Us Pray.

Dear God, I am poor and needy. Remember me today and deliver me from the burden of pursuing social acceptance. Created in me a hunger to do the good I can today.

In Jesus's Name, I pray.

Amen 

Day Twenty-Six

Proverbs 4: 1

'Hear, ye children, the instructions of a father, and attend to know to understand.'

We Often hear young people say, 'That's old school, Dad' Dear child, take time to read the book of Proverbs, and you will begin to think and act differently. The principle of wisdom in every aspect of our daily lives is beautifully outlined in the book of Proverbs. The above verse is one such. You may think your parents are old and not in touch with modern technology, but if you find yourself on a sinking ship with not enough life jacket to go around, that 'old dad" might not only get to the shore but also likely to save someone else who is open to follow his instructions. Why is it so? This is because they have been through such situations before. Fathers may be old but have experienced or heard stories of those who have been through that path which you intend to tread. The most successful people are those humble enough to accept the instructions of parents or elderly persons.

The story is told of a young man, twenty-one years old, who dropped out of college to pursue his "dream' musical career. The father told him how some of his own brothers had dropped out of school for similar reasons at almost the same age. They were now in their fifties. Not only did their dream not materialize, but they were also now stuck with a minimum-wage paying job because that was all they could get with their qualifications. For many years they went from one 'get the rich quick idea' to another without success. The minimum wage could not afford decent housing. They could not take care of their families or even pay for their children's education. They often came to him for assistance which has placed an enormous burden on him. The father pleaded with the son to complete his college degree. The son did not listen. He dropped out of school and moved in with his girlfriend whose family values differs.

It's been five years. The son is now twenty-six years old. And there seems to be no light in sight on the other side of the tunnel. He has been switching from one minimum-wage job to the other. He can neither pay his share of the rented apartment he shares with his girlfriend, who graduated from college, nor pay for his car.

If the young man had listened to his parents and completed college, maybe he could have been earning more than the minimum wage and still be able to pursue his "dream" after graduation at twenty-three.

Let Us Pray.

Dear God, forgive me for the many times I have disregarded and slighted the instructions of my parents. Open my heart and mind to receive the good instructions being offered to me. Bless my parents and all the elders you have positioned around me with the wisdom to lead.

In Jesus's Name Amen 

Day Twenty-Seven

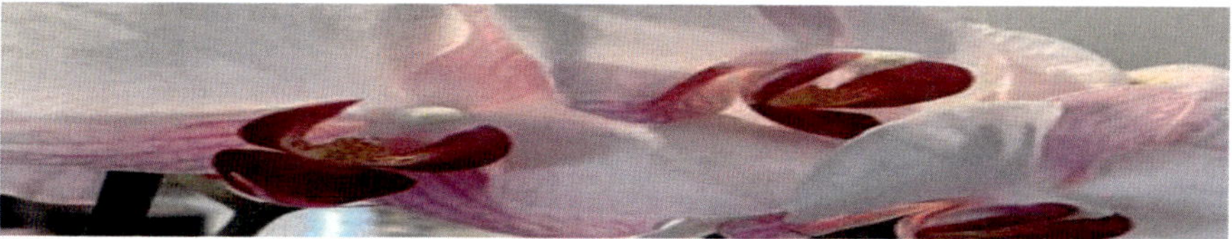

Luke 6: 28

'Bless them that curse you, and pray for them which despitefully use you.'

Hmm! No way. How can I pray to God to bless that wicked coworker who almost got me fired by her lies. Or my ex, who almost drove me mad. God's love is gentle and kind. It overlooks insults and hatred. It is unexplainable. That is why God crowned His son Jesus Christ the King of Kings and Lord of Lords because He blessed those who despised and persecuted Him. He looked up and said, "Father, forgive them, for they know not what they are doing," when He had the power to beckon the angels to destroy His tormentors.

God can change your situation if you bless and pray for your coworker whose lies cost you your dream job; or the ex who, despitefully used you, left you bankrupt and ran away with another person.

There was this young man who landed a job as an engineer in a huge corporation. The young man was ecstatic, being his first job and a high paying one at that. The CEO seemed to like the young man's energy and willingness to learn new skills. One of the coworkers, however, who has been in the organization for over twenty years, disliked him because of the color of his skin. Anytime the young man was paired with him on a project, he would make life unbearable for him. He would either cause unexplainable delays or deliberately delete his files. Some of his antics caused the organization to lose millions of dollars. The young man was mentally drained and contemplating suicide when he accidentally tuned into a radio station on his way home one day. As he listened, he heard the preacher talking about a young man who was contemplating suicide. The preacher went on to say, 'I challenge you today to pray for and bless your coworker who has put you in this mess and see what God will do in your life.' Right there, the young man began to pray for his coworker, and by the time he arrived home, he felt peace which he had not experienced in a long while. He slept like a baby that night

When the young man arrived at work the next day, he was summoned by the CEO to his office. He thought to himself, 'This is it. I am getting fired'. He was terrified. Instead of being fired, here is what the CEO said. "I have watched you closely since you joined this organization. I see you as someone who can take this organization to a higher level. The incident of the past month was unfortunate. For now, I will be sending you to head the new branch in Chicago'. The young man almost fainted.

The preacher saved this young man's life. Today, let us challenge ourselves to do likewise and pray for those who have wronged us and see how God can turn our situation around. It might not be as immediate as it was for this young man. Wait for it. For It will surely come to pass because 'what God cannot do, does not exist.'

Let Us Pray.

Dear God, forgive me for the many times I have doubted your word and failed to follow your instructions. Please, Lord, give me the grace to" Blessed them that curse me and pray for them which despitefully use me.

In Jesus's Name.

Amen 

Day Twenty-Eight

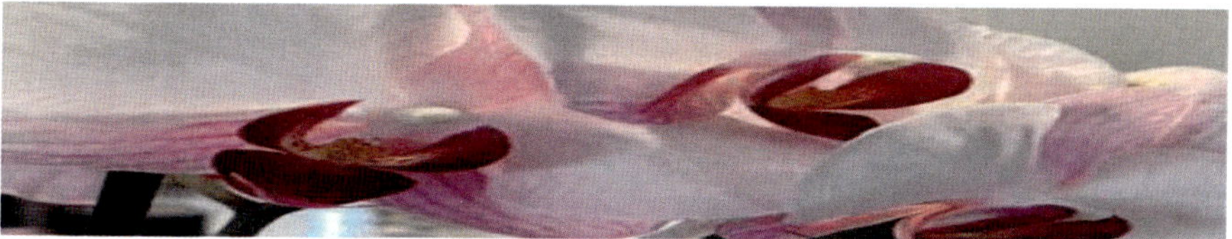

Luke 15: 18

'I will arise and go to my father and will say unto him. Father, I have sinned against heaven and before thee.'

It takes great courage to get to that point of realization which brings inner peace. The story of the prodigal son is still very popular today. Unlike the prodigal son in this Bible verse, pride and shame prevent today's estranged individuals from getting to that point of realization. They are pushed deeper and deeper until they lose every dignity and go into depression and despair. They latch out at anyone who attempts to show them compassion, be they siblings, parents, teachers, neighbors, or pastors. They blame everyone but themselves and listen to the voices of hate and discouragement tormenting them.

We are being reminded today to be courageous enough to say, 'I have wasted valuable time and energy in pursuit of that which was good in my eyes; I will arise and go back home. I do not want to be in this place of mental torture and darkness anymore'.

Dear child come back home; a banquet awaits you. Your father may not be as financially buoyant as the prodigal son's father; He may not be able to kill a calf or hire musicians to celebrate your return, but within his heart, the melody of joy is playing on. Come, come, come home.

Let Us Pray.

Dear God, I am deeply sorry for the many times I failed to follow your will and so offended my parents and the entire family. Give me the courage to get to the point of realization and to say, "I will arise and go to my father and will say unto him. Father, I have sinned against heaven and before thee."

Amen 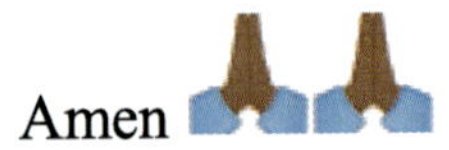

Day Twenty-Nine

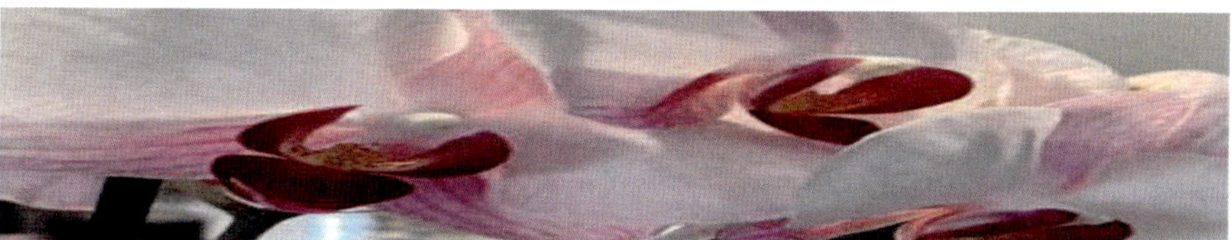

Psalm 71: 1-2

'In your saving, Justice, rescue me, deliver me, listen to me, and save me.'

You and I had echoed this cry for help at some point in our lives when the world seemed to be crashing down on us with no humanly possible way out. Even now, you feel trapped in the situation you are in. You appear to be hedged in with no way out. Here is the thing you must know: Before and when you cry, He knows and hears. Sometimes He says 'YES, at other times, He says 'WAIT,' and of course, in some instances, He says 'NO.' He does know the right time. You may be in an abusive relationship, searching for your dream job but are met each time with 'we are sorry, the job has been offered to a more qualified candidate,' Or you may have a job with a boss who does not appreciate your daily input, Others may be weighed down with relationship issues. Whatever obstacle you may be up against, be reminded today to cry out like the Psalmist in this text. The Lord is telling you today, 'I hear you, my child. I am standing here beside you. I will help you.

Let Us Pray.

Dear Lord, forgive me the many times I have been blind and deaf to the answer to my cry. Open my eyes to see and ears to hear. 'It is going to be alright. Trust me, echoing from your throne.

This I ask in Jesus's Name.

Amen 

Day Thirty

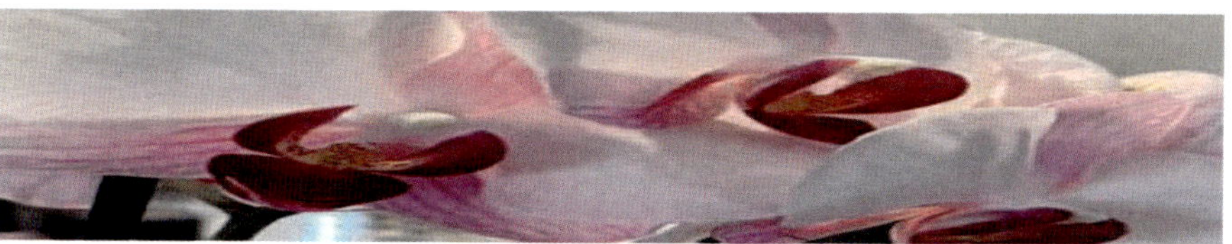

Timothy 4: 12

'But serve as an example to the believers in your speech, conduct, love, faith, and purity.'

Timothy was a youth, as are many of us today. He was a fervent believer, loyal and submissive to God and to Paul, his earthly mentor. Paul was encouraging Timothy to be an example in his ways. Good conduct attracts favor and blessings. It will exonerate you when you are wrongfully accused

A young lady once told a story of how she was called to her boss's office and informed of his imminent retirement from active business. According to the young lady, the boss handed over the reins of the business to her. The boss told the young lady how he had been observing her conduct over the years. He felt she had been tested and proven to be fit to head his business. Little did she know that the boss had been testing her those times he left unsigned invoices worth millions of dollars to see if she would alter the figures. Stacks of cash have also been left unattended in her office at various times, and not a dime had gone missing. Yes, good conduct and integrity will uphold you. Today she controls the multi-million-dollar business for the boss.

Dear child, good things still happen to people who conduct themselves in a godly way.

Let Us Pray.

Dear God, forgive me for the many times I have failed to conduct myself according to your will. Grant me the grace to stay steadfast no matter how difficult my situation may be. Help me and the youth to recognize the blessings and favors gained from churning greed. Bless all young adults in their daily struggles.

In Jesus's Name, I pray

Amen 

Made in the USA
Monee, IL
23 May 2023